I0520796

From the lights to the LAMB

Amber Whiteaker

ODDO creations
www.ODDOcreations.com

Copyright © 2025 by Amber Whiteaker

Published in Olive Branch, Mississippi by ODDO creations. www.ODDOcreations.com

All rights reserved. Activity pages may be reproduced for your immediate family members only. Otherwise, no portion of this book may be reproduced, stored, or transmitted in any form without prior written permission from the publisher or author, except as permitted by U.S. copyright law. The only exception is brief quotations in reviews.

For printable activity pages for classroom or group use, please contact the author directly through her website at www.AmberWhiteaker.com.

Scripture quotations are taken from the Holy Scriptures, Tree of Life Version*. Copyright © 2014, 2016 by the Tree of Life Bible Society. Used by permission of the Tree of Life Bible Study.

*"TLV" and "Tree of Life Version" and "Tree of Life Holy Scriptures" are trademarks registered in the United States Patent and Trademark office by the Messianic Jewish Family Bible Society (DBA Tree of Life Bible Society).

Cover Design by ODDO creations at www.ODDOcreations.com

ISBN 979-8-9936883-0-5

For Madison, Paxton, Bella, and Emerson

You are my motivation for persevering.

CONTENTS

ACKNOWLEDGMENTS

Immense thanks to my husband, Corey. You patiently put up with my moodiness after sleepless nights and pick up the slack so I can pursue any dream Abba plants in my heart. You are my right arm, and I couldn't do any of this without you. I love you!

To my mentor, Rabbi Jenn Batya, I am blessed to call you my soul sister and precious friend. Thank you for your endless encouragement, reminders of Hashem's faithfulness, and late night cry sessions when I am overwhelmed. You taught me to dig for diamonds, and I cannot begin to express my gratitude for your guidance through the Word. I love doing life with you.

Thank you to my Torah table talk family—Meli, Nathalie, Esther, Gina, and all of the other ladies and families who join us from time to time—for your faithfulness in studying Torah alongside me and for your constant desire to grow closer to the heart of Adonai. I love you all.

To Dolores, you have walked through over half of my life with me, and I'm grateful for your friendship, counsel, and love. You are so precious to me.

To Rabbi Daniel and my *mishpocha* at Beth Israel JMI Hawaii, thank you for your diligence in teaching biblical truth from a Hebraic perspective and for loving and accepting me as one of your own—even though I don't get to visit very often. You are part of my heart forever.

Thank you to my dear sisters who have always been my life's greatest earthly support system. Diane, Elizabeth, and Angela, I love you all so much!

And to my mom, Lisa, you have helped me through every part of this project and are a huge part of its successful completion. Thank you for believing in me, loving me through thick and thin, and encouraging me to always keep growing. I am so grateful that you kept me close to His Word and Truth growing up. I love you, Mommy!

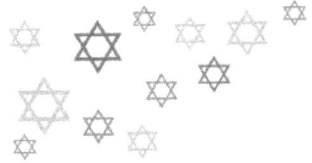
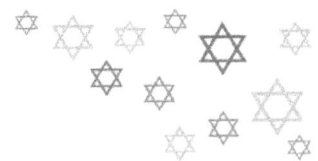

PREFACE

As a mom, I strive to teach my children to be the best versions of themselves. Part of that, if not the majority, lands in the arena of their spiritual growth and mindset. Our culture often pushes commercialism and selfishness, especially during the holiday season. Despite my best efforts, my children are not immune to the surrounding societal customs.

I aspire not to follow any tradition without doing my best to understand the "why" behind it and whether it is biblical. In studying the celebration of Hanukkah, I discovered scripture only mentions this Festival of Lights once. John 10:22-30 is the only appearance of Hanukkah in the entire Bible, and it sets the scene in which Yeshua verbally affirms Himself as Messiah to the Jewish leaders. Color me shocked!

I believe if Yeshua celebrated or honored it, so should I. So, we added Hanukkah to our holiday season. Unfortunately, many celebration ideas led my children to expect treats and gifts rather than focus on the true reason for the season—learning to give instead of "get" and to share the Light of Adonai with the world. Because I want our celebrations focused on biblical truth, I searched for ways to refocus the holidays for our family. Finding very little that truly blended the seasonal festivities while honoring Hebraic thought, I dug into both Scripture and history, discovering far more unexpected connections along the way.

Thus, this book of eight nightly readings was born. If you want to refocus your family during this holiday season, this book is for you. Keep reading if you seek deeper meaning, scriptural truth that honors Hebraic tradition, and biblical connections that point to Messiah. If you yearn to see the Light in this season of celebrations, whether you celebrate Hanukkah, Christmas, or both, set aside time on each of these nights to discover what (and maybe who) links everything together.

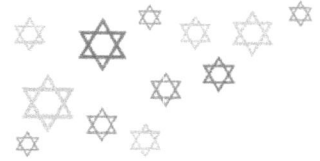
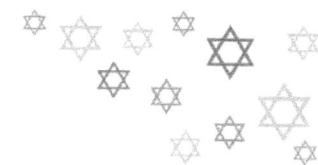

NIGHT I

BE HUMBLE LIKE THE DONKEY

We begin this night lighting the *shamash* or "helper" candle. Once this candle is lit, it assumes the responsibility of lighting each of the candles on the Hanukkah menorah, also known as the *Hanukkiah*. It is plain and humble, but it shares light for all eight nights of Hanukkah. Likewise, we should reflect humility during this season of light. From here, we illuminate the world. We miss out on opportunities to brighten our surroundings if, in our pride, we cannot humble ourselves. From a place of service, we are most able to see other's needs and subsequently meet them. We have the responsibility to become "helpers" to those we encounter.

As we enter the eight nights of Hanukkah, take a moment to consider the number eight and how it might connect to the idea of humility. Throughout Scripture, the number eight represents new beginnings, covenant, and purification. Noah's ark only carried eight people through the floodwaters to establish life anew on the earth (Genesis 7:7, 1 Peter 3:20). On the eighth day of a baby's life, circumcision served as a sign of the covenant between Abraham and Adonai (Genesis 17:11-12). Hezekiah spent eight days purifying the temple after his father had made it a place of idolatry (2 Chronicles 29:17).

How do new beginnings, covenant, and purification relate to humility? Much like the Holy Temple rededication in 164 BCE mentioned in the Hanukkah story, this is a time to come before Adonai in humility, ask Him to purify our hearts, renew our covenant promises to remain faithful to Him, and to start the next season with fresh perspective and dedication. This is our time to commit "to walk humbly with [our] God" (Micah 6:8 TLV).

We can take our cue from one of the humblest animals mentioned in the Word of God—the donkey. Like the *shamash* candle, the donkey humbly carries its responsibilities from one place to another. In Genesis 22:3, a donkey carries the supplies for sacrifice when Abraham journeys to the mountain with Isaac to offer his only son as a sacrifice to Adonai. A donkey carries provisions from Joseph for his brothers in Genesis 42:26-28, and in chapter 44, it carries back the means to restore a right relationship with the brother they wronged years prior. Exodus 4:20 tells of the donkey which carries Moses and his family to Egypt to begin God's deliverance of His people. In 1 Samuel 16:20, a donkey carries David to his new position as a servant to King Saul.

The prophet Zechariah proclaims, "Behold, your king is coming to you, a righteous one bringing salvation. He is lowly, riding on a donkey—on a colt, the foal of a donkey" (Zechariah 9:9).

And while the Bible doesn't specifically mention a donkey in the nativity story, it is likely one carried a young girl named Mary with a very special baby in her womb.

The Hebrew word for donkey is *chamor*. The first letter of that word is *chet*, which is the eighth letter of the Hebrew alphabet.

During these eight nights of Hanukkah, and especially as we light the first candles on the *Hanukkiah*, may we find ourselves humbled in reflecting upon the donkey, which carried the only Son—the renewed covenant—who would become the pure sacrifice of salvation. He provides for our restoration to Adonai and delivers us from all that seeks to hold us captive, so we can make a fresh start in service to Him, the King of kings who fulfilled the prophecy of Zechariah when He later rode into Jerusalem on the back of a donkey to the cries of "*Baruch ha-ba b'shem Adonai*! Blessed is He who comes in the name of the Lord!" (Matthew 21:9).

Family Discussion Questions

(You may write your answers here or in a journal to compare them year after year. Encourage all family members to take part and reassure them no answer is wrong.)

What are some practical ways you can be a *shamash*, or helper, in your family?

Where in your life do you feel you need a fresh start?

What does the word "covenant" mean to you?

Is there a burden you feel might be too heavy for you to carry?

Family Prayer Time

(You can use mine or pray in your own words.)

Blessed are you, Adonai our God, King of the Universe and Creator of new beginnings. We humble ourselves before You tonight with a desire to renew our heart connection to Yours. We want to honor You with our words, thoughts, and actions as we seek to serve others. Thank You for keeping your commitment and covenant with us for all of eternity and for renewing that commitment through Your only Son. We praise You for Your faithfulness! In the name of Yeshua, we pray. Amen.

SHAMASH FOR A DAY ACTIVITY BOX

1. Decorate a small box or other small container with a lid.
2. Think of ways you can be a "Shamash," or helper, in your family.
3. Write your ideas on the candles below. Then, cut them out to put in your box.
4. Draw out a candle each morning and do that activity throughout the day. (Note: If you have a big family, take turns being the "Shamash for the day" or use activities everyone can do together for others in your area.)

Use the chart to decipher the hidden message.

A= 🕎	B= 🎁	C= 🍇	D= 🌙	E= ✳	F= ✡	G= ❄
H= ⬆	I= ☀	J= 🐟	K= 🧿	L= 📖	M= ◇	N= 👑
O= ☺	P= 🌈	Q= ⬡	R= △	S= ♡	T= ✝	U= 🔥
V= 🎀	W= ✶	X= ✚	Y= ★	Z= ☁		

FOR EVEN THE SON OF MAN DID

NOT COME TO BE SERVED, BUT

TO SERVE, AND TO GIVE HIS

LIFE AS A RANSOM FOR MANY

MARK 10:45

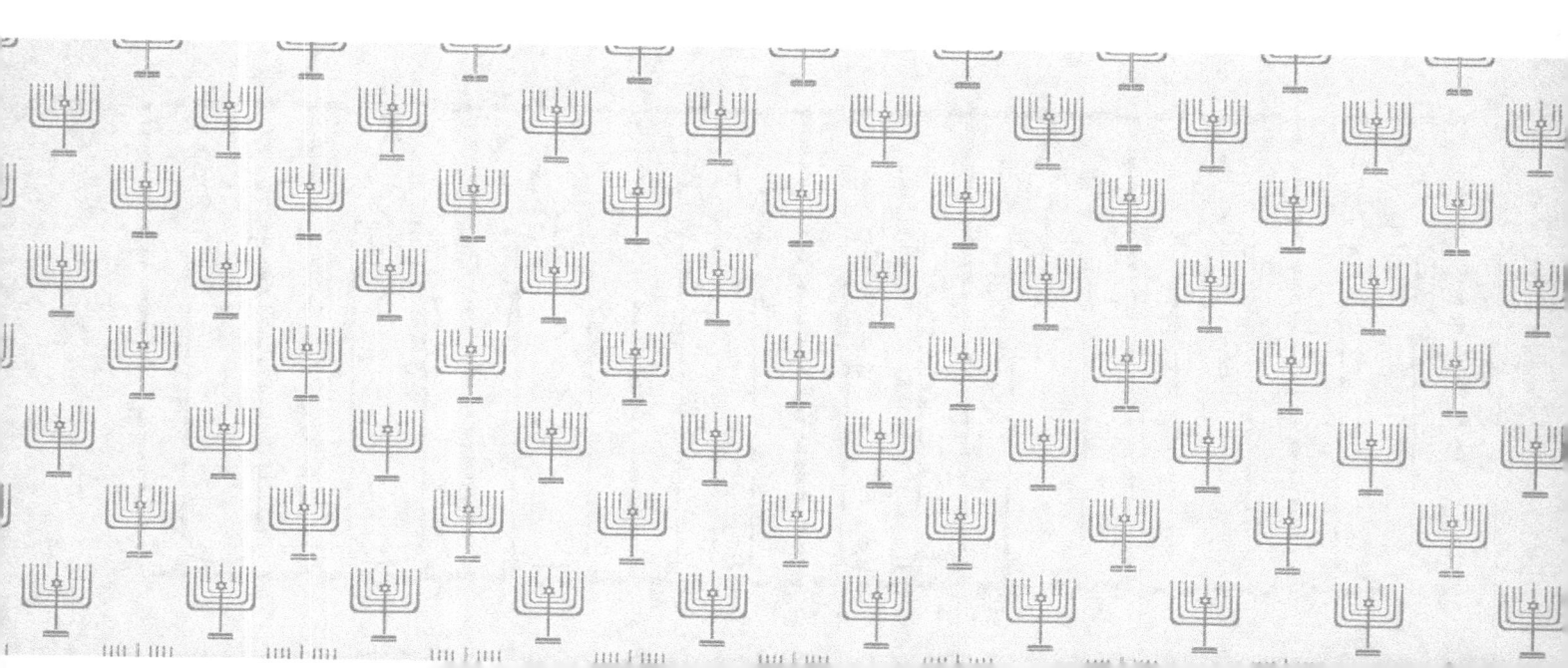

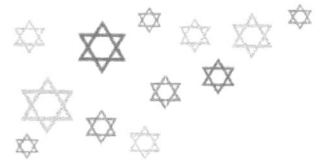
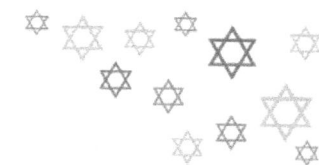

NIGHT 2

WORSHIP LIKE JOSEPH

On this second night of Hanukkah, we once again light the *shamash* and note its purpose. This candle stands ready to reignite any flame that extinguishes on the *Hanukkiah*. This quiet act of service mimics our purpose as light bearers to the world. When we encounter someone whose light has dimmed or succumbed to the darkness, it is our responsibility to remind them of the true Light Source and help restore their glow. Rekindling the light in others is our act of worship in service to Adonai. It is our duty to dispel the darkness by spreading the light.

In the Hanukkah story, when Antiochus IV Epiphanes controlled Jerusalem, he not only forbade all Jewish practices but also set up sacrificial altars to his pagan deities. In the place where the people should have only worshiped Adonai, the Syrian Greeks performed their pagan sacrifices on the Holy Altar! This false worship was loud and bold—nothing like the *shamash*—and the darkness seemed all-consuming. However, once Judah Maccabees and his small army restored and purified the temple, worship and prayer took precedence. Lighting the candle on the temple menorah became an act of worship, a light to dispel the darkness of all the false worship previously filling that place. After lighting the candle, they celebrated in the manner of Sukkot—singing Psalms of worship and thanksgiving, praying for continued deliverance, and thanking Him for restoration to their holy land and of His holy place.

Theologian Bruce Leafblad defines worship as what happens when we "set our mind's attention and heart's affection on the Lord."[1] These are internal activities, not external displays. In the nativity story, Joseph displayed this kind of pure, quiet worship when he chose not to shame Mary upon discovering her pregnancy. When we read the brief snippet of his story told in the gospels of Matthew and Luke, we can see his similarity to the *shamash*. When Adonai sends an angel to Joseph in his dreams, he acts immediately. He listens to and takes Adonai at His word and then responds accordingly. This is akin to the *shamash* and its availability to act quickly to reignite a waning or burned out flame.

Had Joseph not heeded Adonai's warnings and fled to Egypt immediately, Herod would have snuffed out the Light of Messiah (Matthew 2:14). Joseph's faithful obedience to Torah also ensured Adonai's promises to others. Revelation to Shim'on (Simeon) assured him "he would not die before he had seen the Messiah of Adonai" (Luke 2:26). Because Joseph and Mary took Yeshua to the temple for purification, as the law of Moses required, Adonai fulfilled this promise to Shim'on.

While they were there, Hannah (Anna), of the tribe of Asher (one of the lost tribes of Israel), would serve as a second legal witness to acknowledge Yeshua's role as redeemer of Israel and, subsequently, the entire lost world.[2] Joseph, a righteous man, worshipped Adonai with his life. His quiet obedience fulfilled prophecy after prophecy and kept aflame the boy, Yeshua, until He was old enough to know Torah and begin teaching others—spreading the Light on His own.

As we light the second candle on our *Hanukkiah* tonight, may we remember to worship Adonai like Joseph, in the quiet places of our hearts and minds. May our actions reflect our obedience to His Word. Let us quickly move to reignite the flames of those we encounter whose light has faltered or the enemy has snuffed out. Above all, remember to keep your light burning brightly, so we always remain prepared to kindle and rekindle the flame in others. Let us ensure the darkness remains far away.

Family Discussion Questions

(You may write your answers here or in a journal to compare them year after year. Encourage all family members to take part and reassure them no answer is wrong.)

Can you think of someone who seems to walk in darkness or sadness? You don't need to name them, but what are some ways you can help rekindle their light?

Do you have a favorite worship song? Play it now and worship together.

How can you better focus your mind and heart on Adonai?

Do you have any darkness in your life? Help each other return to the Light of Adonai.

Family Prayer Time

(You can use mine or pray in your own words.)

Blessed are you, Adonai our God, King of the Universe and Giver of Light. Thank You for shining brightly and never dimming Your Light. We ask You to reveal areas of darkness in our home, family, and surroundings so we can bring them back into the light of Your love and truth. When we struggle, please give us courage to seek help from You and from those who love us. We want to worship You in the quiet places of our hearts. In the name of Yeshua, we pray. Amen.

Complete the other half of the Hanukkiah.

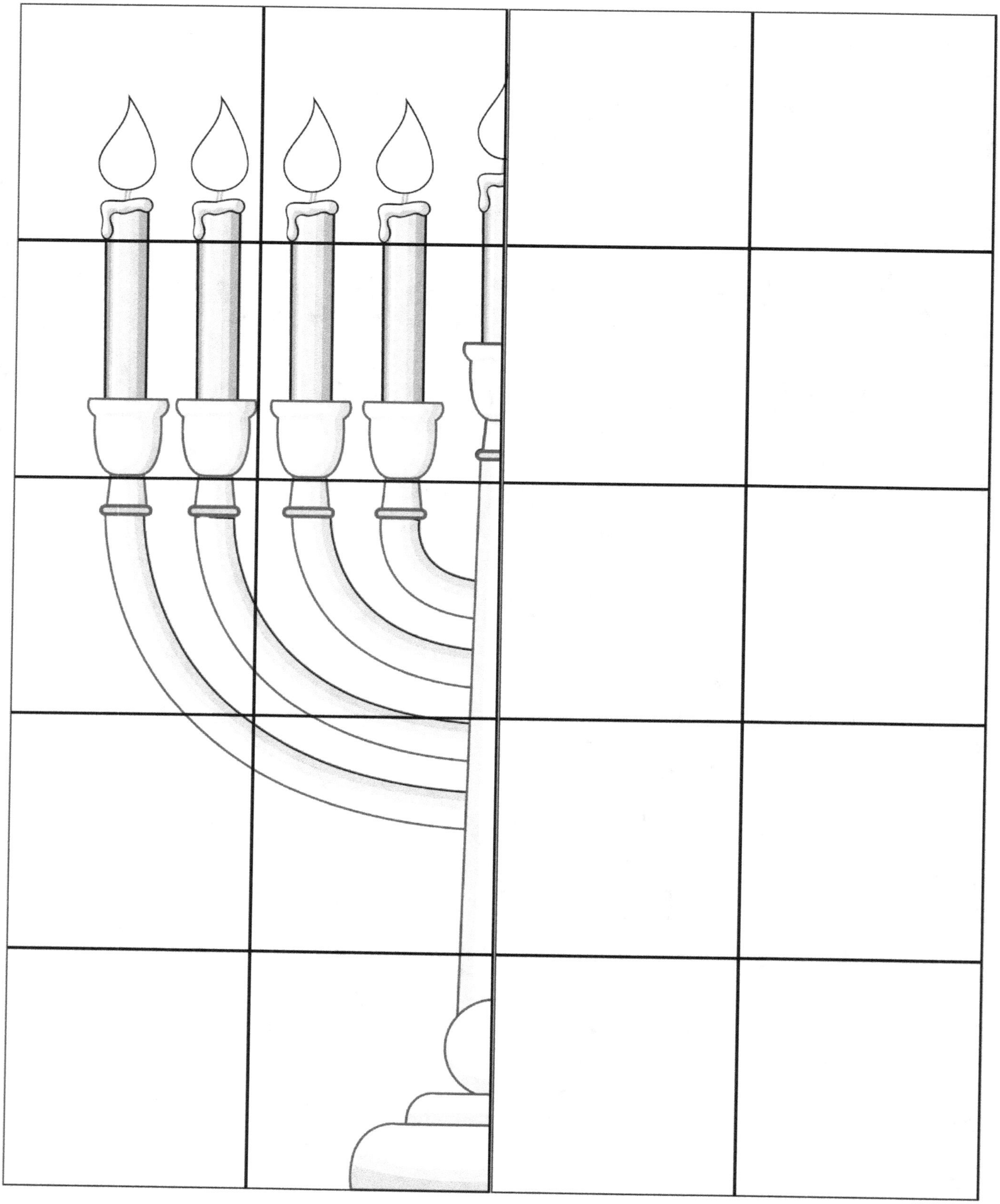

Find the hidden words in the box below.

```
C A H X T B E T O O S W D S S X G F Z N
W A K I N D L E V Q O M N H V Z G M I Z
O U N P V P X U J G Q A J X V U Y Q C M
R C A D E R W B D Z T T Y M M J Q F B W
S F S A L H T L Y B I A U P W U I I N B
H Z A B C E F O S P E T V R Q E Y H W
I O Q L H L Y R A C Q W G O X E J R V D
P K P B D U B S N L B X K P D J S Z L A
J E L K T O V A K O A X V H F H H A M H
D Z L P L U R Q I R G N I E X D U Q Q A
S P F X T E J B V Z D C E C H W A H M N
L K L J V K J Q C B V T R Y D Q S B A U
O F P I H B A K F F O F A M I A R E C K
S B L I W S O N E B K P B E M N N I C K
R E S T O R A T I O N S A A C O A U A I
D F D G R I F P B O A H H R E U V N B A
Z D X J A U T T V S H S O I J R T D E H
T J B B L I G H T K K S P G J S E P E C
M K O F L A M E V C U W S T I N T N S N
K D M I R M A W Y H I C F U L O V E H H
```

PROPHECY   MACCABEES   KINDLE

SHAMASH   RESTORATION   YESHUA

WORSHIP   DELIVERANCE   LIGHT

CANDLE   HANUKKIAH   FLAME

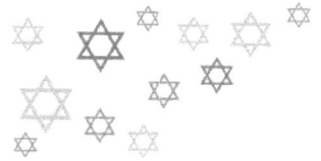
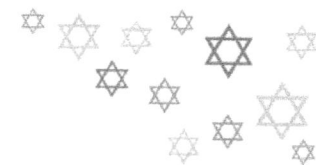

NIGHT 3

OWN YOUR LINEAGE LIKE MARY

On this third night of Hanukkah, the *Hanukkiah* reminds us of another menorah—the one in the Holy Temple. This menorah served as a reminder of God's presence among His people. The person responsible for lighting this lampstand is the *kohen gadol*, or high priest. Adonai assigned this job to Aaron and his descendants in the wilderness when He established the design for His dwelling place, the Tabernacle. They kindled each flame and kept it burning consistently to provide light. The *kohen* also carried the responsibility of mediator between the people and Adonai. He offered sacrifices on their behalf, ensuring their cleanliness before Him.

One such *kohen gadol* is a central figure in the Hanukkah story. His name was Mattathias. The Jews who joined in the Hellenistic practices in the temple grieved him greatly. The dark part of the Hanukkah story is in the civil war between the Jews who remained faithful to Torah and those who ignored it in favor of the societal pressures surrounding them. Judah Maccabees, Mattathias' son, assembled other faithful followers to reclaim the Temple for Adonai. He took on the role of a priestly deliverer of the Jewish populace. In his success, the *kohanim* were once again able to kindle the menorah's light.

This may not seem to relate to the nativity story, but Mary is the one who ties everything together. Scripture doesn't specifically attribute any lineage to Mary. However, most scholars agree the genealogy found in the book of Luke belongs to Mary. This lineage differs from that found in Matthew, which traces Joseph's ancestry back to King David through his son, Solomon, to Judah and further on to Abraham. This follows his paternal and kingly heritage in the way the Jews would have recognized and responded. Luke, who wrote primarily to a gentile audience, traced Yeshua's ancestry biologically all the way back through King David's son, Nathan, and continued to Adam, the first son of God's creation. In this lineage, we also find Shem, who was Noah's oldest son. We know God rescued Noah because of his righteousness. That righteousness would have passed down to Shem, his firstborn son. While debate remains, some Rabbinic opinions claim Shem may have been the same person as Melchizedek[3], meaning "my king of righteousness." In Psalm 110:4, David reiterates his own lineage of "kohen forever according to the order of Melchizedek," and the author of Hebrews later attributes this same title to Yeshua Jesus. Melchizedek was a *kohen* before Aaron, not made by Torah law but by the "virtue of the power of an indestructible life" (Hebrews 7:16).

Mary's lineage carries not only the biological line directly to God but also defines Yeshua's role as the priestly deliverer of the Jews and the entire world. He is our *kohen gadol*, the one who mediates for us before Adonai and ensures our cleanliness forever through His sacrifice. He is the One who kindles the light of our lives and keeps the flame burning not just for the evening and morning but for all eternity.

As we light the third candle on the *Hanukkiah* tonight, let us remember the words in 1 Peter 2:4-5 and 9. "As you come to Him, a living stone rejected by men but chosen by God and precious, you also, as living stones, are being built up as a spiritual house—a holy priesthood to offer up spiritual sacrifices acceptable to God through Messiah Yeshua...You are a chosen people, a royal priesthood, a holy nation, a people for God's own possession, so that you may proclaim the praises of the One who called you out of darkness into His marvelous light."

It is our job to kindle the light like the *kohen* of old because we, too, are a royal priesthood in and through Yeshua Jesus.

Family Discussion Questions

(You may write your answers here or in a journal to compare them year after year. Encourage all family members to take part and reassure them no answer is wrong.)

What are the responsibilities of a *kohen*?

How was Judah Maccabees a priestly deliverer to the Jews?

Why is it important to trace Joseph's lineage to King David **and** Mary's lineage all the way to Adam? What does that mean for their Son, Yeshua?

What are some practical ways you can carry out the responsibilities of a *kohen*?

Family Prayer Time

(You can use mine or pray in your own words.)

Blessed are you, Adonai our God, King of the Universe and our Kohen Gadol. Thank You for teaching us how to be the hands and feet of Yeshua. We pray for wisdom and guidance as we represent You to the world. Give us grace for ourselves and each other as we strive toward righteousness within and reflect the Light out onto those we encounter. In the name of Yeshua, we pray. Amen.

Therefore encourage one another
and build each other up.
1 Thessalonians 5:11

Find the hidden words below.

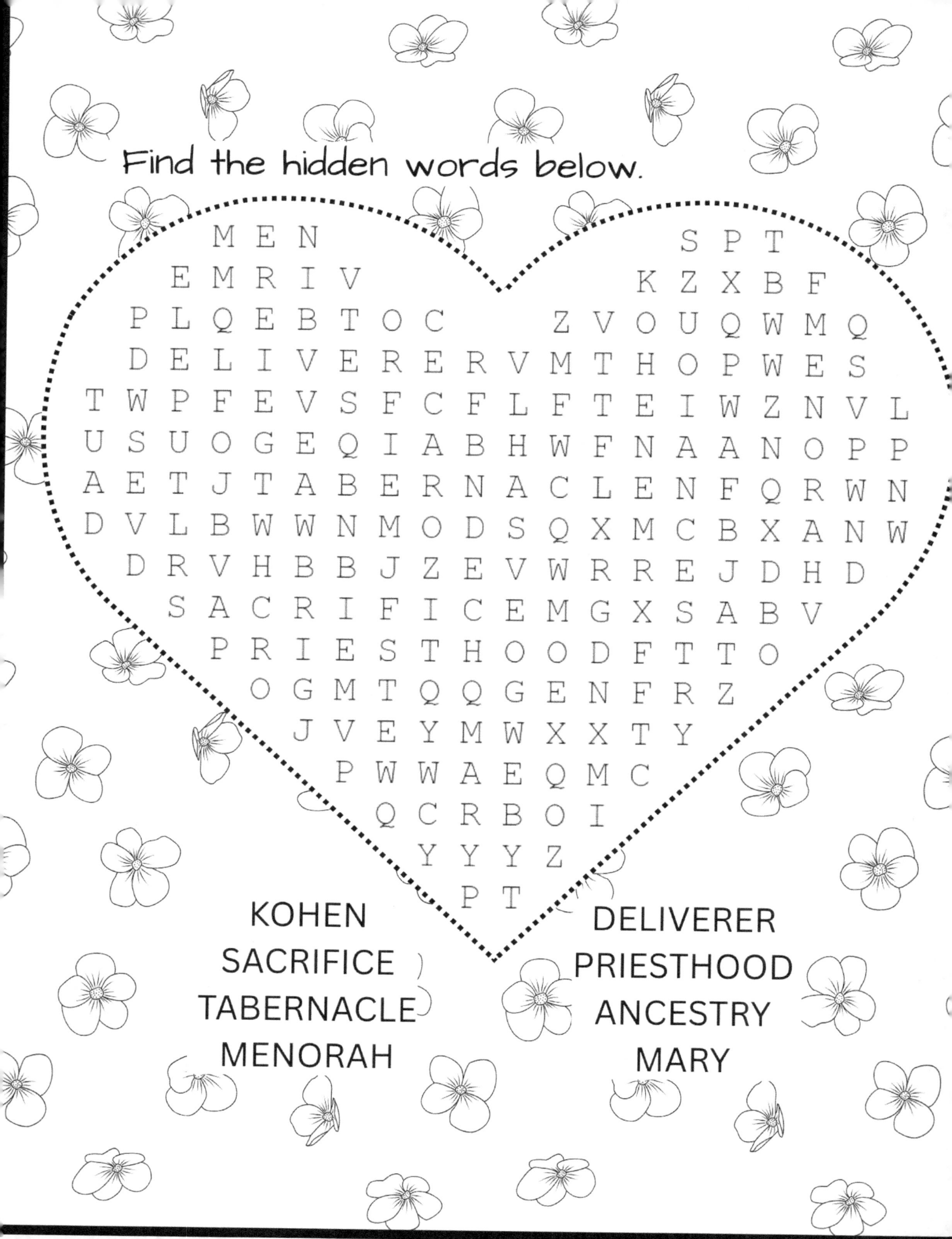

```
        M E N                          S P T
      E M R I V                      K Z X B F
    P L Q E B T O C              Z V O U Q W M Q
    D E L I V E R E R V M T H O P W E S
  T W P F E V S F C L F T E I W Z N V L
  U S U O G E Q I A B H W F N A A N O P P
  A E T J T A B E R N A C L E N F Q R W N
  D V L B W W N M O D S Q X M C B X A N W
    D R V H B B J Z E V W R R E J D H D
    S A C R I F I C E M G X S A B V
      P R I E S T H O O D F T T O
      O G M T Q Q G E N F R Z
      J V E Y M W X X T Y
        P W W A E Q M C
        Q C R B O I
          Y Y Y Z
            P T
```

KOHEN

SACRIFICE

TABERNACLE

MENORAH

DELIVERER

PRIESTHOOD

ANCESTRY

MARY

Color the breastplate for the kohen according to the numbers below.

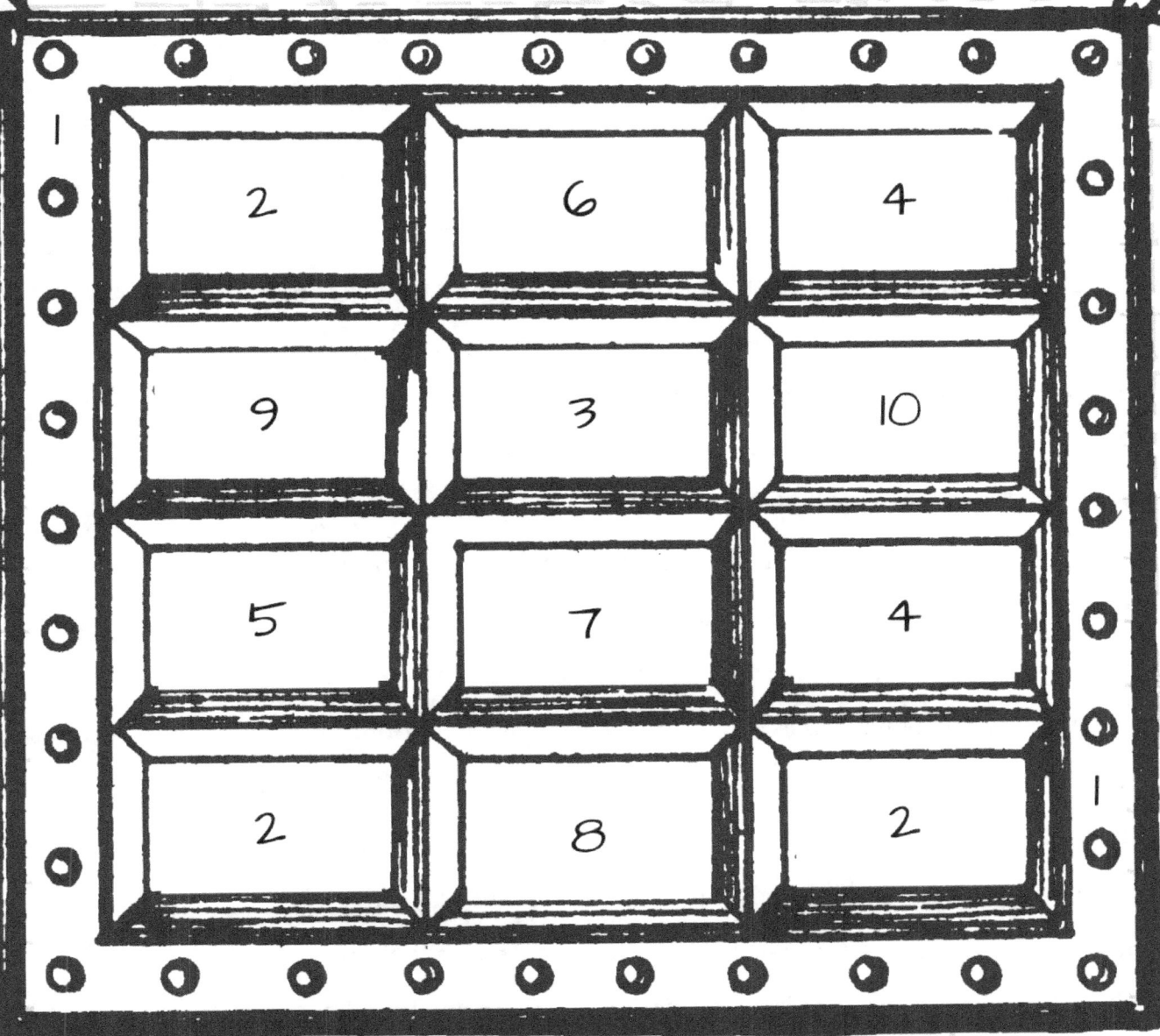

1 - Yellow 2 - Green 3 - Blue 4 - Red
5 - Purple 6 - Orange 7 - Pink 8 - Black
9 - Grey 10 - Turquoise

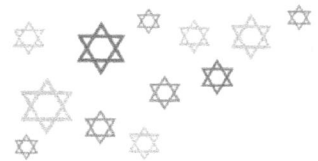
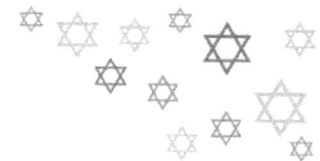

NIGHT 4

ILLUMINATE LIKE THE STAR

The purpose of the *Hanukkiah* on our tables and the menorah in the temple is the same—to shine a light in the darkness. The menorah in the temple represented the Divine Light of Adonai. It illuminated only the area in front of the menorah, there in the inner court nearest to Adonai's presence. It did not shine out into the world by design but only for those acting in service to Him. Isaiah prophesied about a time when many would flock to Adonai's House to learn from Him and walk in His paths. "Come house of Jacob, let us walk in the light of Adonai" (Isaiah 2:5). To walk in His divine light, one needs to draw near to Him.

During Hanukkah, it is imperative that we do not hide our light but set it on a windowsill or similar place, allowing it to shine out into the world. Isaiah also reminded the people it was too big of a job for them to restore the tribes of Jacob and the remnant of Israel on their own. Instead, Adonai said, "...I will give You as a light for the nations, that You should be My salvation to the end of the earth" (Isaiah 49:6b). The purpose of the *Hanukkiah* is to be a symbol to the nations of His salvation and light. It is our job to take the truth of His Word from the place where we are closest to His presence and illuminate it for the rest of the world to see.

There is a light in the Nativity story that somewhat steals the show, although it was only truly significant to a group of Gentiles. The star in the night sky over Bethlehem first appeared on the night of Yeshua's birth. It was likely not a super bright alignment of planets or a comet shooting across the sky, because those things would have been extremely noticeable to everyone in Jerusalem, including King Herod and the temple leaders in that day. However, it was a new star, like a nova or supernova perhaps, one unnoticed before. Those who looked for it are the ones who saw it when it appeared. Why were they looking? Perhaps prophecies from foreign lands played a role. 1400 years earlier, Balaam, a Mesopotamian prophet, spoke Adonai's blessings over the Hebrews in the wilderness. "...For a star will come from Jacob, a scepter will arise from Israel" (Numbers 24:19). Learned men from foreign lands would have known about a king, a scepter, coming from Israel to crush the enemies of Adonai.

In Babylon, Daniel prophesied there would be 483 years[4] between "the issuing of the decree to restore and to build Jerusalem until the time *Mashiach*, the Prince" comes (Daniel 9:25). Both Jewish and Christian scholars may debate the official start of that prophecy, but most agree that by the time of Yeshua's birth, most of those years (or sabbatical cycles[5]) had passed. Those who knew Daniel's prophecy would have been expecting the one who would fulfill it. It was a combination of prophecies from outside nations that drew the attention of the non-Jewish people. The star was the light to the nations, announcing Yeshua, Adonai's gift of "salvation to the end of the earth."

In Matthew 5:14-16, Yeshua said, "You are the light of the world. A city set on a hill cannot be hidden. Neither do people light a lamp and put it under a basket. Instead, they put it on a lampstand so it gives light to all in the house. In the same way, let your light shine before men so they may see your good works and glorify your Father in heaven."

As we light the fourth Hanukkah candle, may we remember to draw close to the One whose birth the star illuminated, and may we shine forth His Divine Light to the nations like the *Hanukkiah* in our windows.

Family Discussion Questions

(You may write your answers here or in a journal to compare them year after year. Encourage all family members to take part and reassure them no answer is wrong.)

How can we experience the light of Adonai?

What does placing the *Hanukkiah* on the windowsill represent? What are some practical ways we can shine light out to the world?

Why is it significant that people who were not Jews knew about the birth of Yeshua?

How can we show kinship with both Jewish and non-Jewish believers?

Family Prayer Time

(You can use mine or pray in your own words.)

Blessed are you, Adonai our God, King of the Universe and Master Gardener. Thank You for grafting all believers in Yeshua into Your family tree. We ask for Your shalom to grace every interaction between Jewish and non-Jewish believers since we are all one in You. Help us draw close to You so that we can shine with the truth of Your Word. In the name of Yeshua, we pray. Amen.

Find the path to bring your light to the world.

SHINE YOUR LIGHT

Your word is a lamp to my feet and a light to my path.
Psalm 119:105

And the Word became flesh and tabernacled among us.
John 1:14

Color the Hanukkiah in the window according to the letters below.

A - Yellow B - Blue C - Red D - Purple
E - Green F - Orange G - Pink

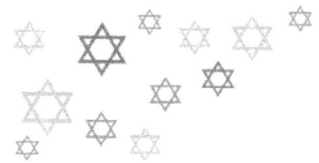
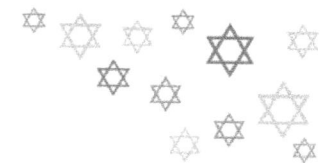

NIGHT 5

SHARE BOLDLY LIKE ANGELS

Sometimes shining the light means sacrificing our comfort and bravely declaring we belong to Adonai. It is worth noting the menorah's symbolic representation of Torah, the Word of the Lord. Standing in front of the menorah allows the light of His Word to illuminate our lives. The *Hanukkiah* is also a type of menorah and should remind us to share Adonai's truth to illuminate the lives of others. Spreading the Light of the Word takes courage, but we can echo the cries of David from Psalm 27:1. "Adonai is my light and my salvation: whom should I fear?" We need not fear because He is the One who sends and guards us along the way.

One of the oldest, most cherished traditions in Jewish heritage and culture is passing down the knowledge of Adonai's law from generation to generation. In the time of Antiochus IV Epiphanes' rule, the law forbade all Jewish practice and Torah study. According to legend, brave children would hide in caves to continue their studies. When the Greek officials patrolled nearby, the children would quickly hide their activities and pull out spinning tops, which we know as dreidels.

The letters on each face of the modern dreidel are nun, gimel, hey, and shin. They stand for *Nes gadol hayah sham*, which means "a great miracle happened there." Further symbolism in the letters is *nefesh* (soul), *guf* (body), *sechel* (understanding), and *hakol* (everything)—words to represent every aspect of a human being.[6] We could interpret this as a reminder of the *Shema*—to "Love Adonai your God with all your heart and with all your soul and with all your understanding" (Deuteronomy 6:5). Regardless of the truth of the popular legend, facing societal or political pressure to hide our light takes courage. We must fearlessly pass down to each generation the command to love Him with everything we have within us.

In scripture, angels often act as Adonai's mouthpiece. The prophecy given to Daniel, which we read about yesterday, came from the angel Gabriel. This same angel visited a young virgin named Mary to disclose her impending supernatural pregnancy and the soon-coming birth of Messiah Yeshua. His name is a shortened form of the name Yehoshua (Joshua), which means "YHWH is Salvation" or "God's Salvation." We would call Him Immanuel, which translates to "God with us" and could further break down to mean "Almighty God is for all of us."

These angelic words fulfilled the prophecy from Isaiah 7:14. "Therefore Adonai Himself will give you a sign: Behold, the virgin will conceive. When she is giving birth to a son, she will call his name Immanuel."

Each time an angel appeared, whether it was to Daniel, Zechariah, Mary, Joseph, or the shepherds in the fields, one of the first things it spoke was "Do not be afraid." When Adonai entrusts us to spread His Word, it can feel a little frightening. Remember the angel's command not to be afraid, and go be a messenger for Adonai.

Isaiah 9:1 proclaims, "The people walking in darkness will see a great light. Upon those dwelling in the land of the shadow of death, light will shine."

John later writes in his gospel account, "In the beginning was the Word. The Word was with God, and the Word was God...In Him was life, and the life was the light of men. The light shines in the darkness, and the darkness has not overpowered it...The true light, coming into the world, gives light to every man" (John 1:1, 4-5, 9). Yeshua was born as the Word, Torah, made into flesh to be the Light which the darkness will never overpower. This world is full of people heading toward spiritual death—eternal separation from Adonai. They need to see the glorious light we know because of Yeshua, who is Salvation, the Menorah, the Word from the beginning of time. As we light the fifth candle, let's remember to be His bold, fearless mouthpiece to humanity and all generations.

Family Discussion Questions

(You may write your answers here or in a journal to compare them year after year. Encourage all family members to take part and reassure them no answer is wrong.)

Why is it important to read the Word of Adonai?

Do you know the *Shema* from Deuteronomy 6:5? Sing or recite it together.

What is something you fear? Can you find scripture together to help replace that fear with truth?

Can you think of someone with whom you want to share the Word of Adonai?

Family Prayer Time

(You can use mine or pray in your own words.)

Blessed are you, Adonai our God, King of the Universe and the Word of Truth. We acknowledge Yeshua as Your Torah, Your Word, made flesh. We ask you to help us know Him better as we study Your truth in scripture. Thank You for helping us be bold and courageous about sharing Your love with our friends. Show them Your Light through our words and actions. In the name of Yeshua, we pray. Amen.

Write a letter to a friend or family member
to share the Light of Adonai with them.
Cut it out and give it to them.

Dear _____,

_____

_____

_____

_____

_____

_____

_____

_____

_____

_____

Love,

_____

Match the letters found on the dreidels
with the words they represent.
Hint: There are two matches for each.

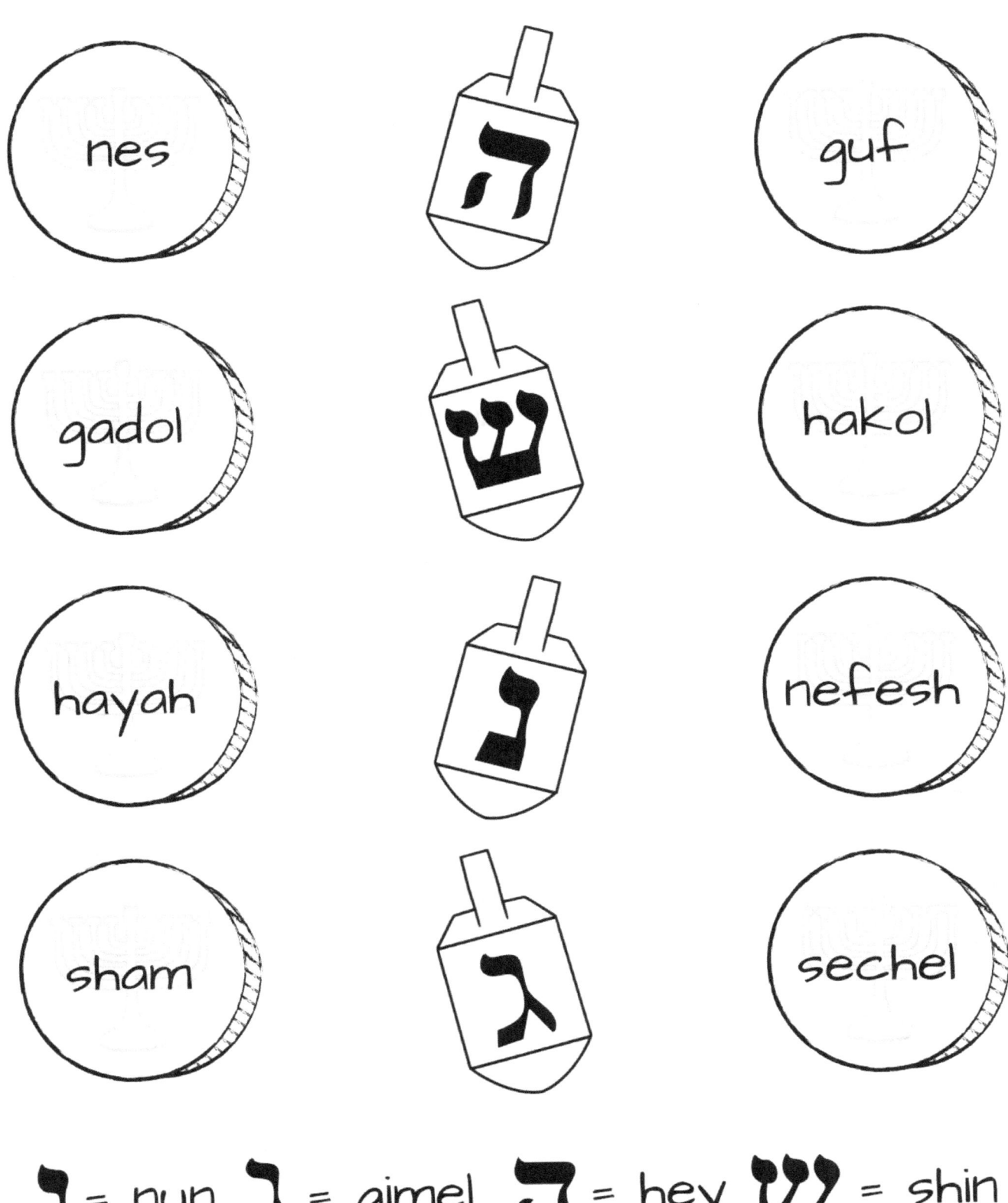

nes

guf

gadol

hakol

hayah

nefesh

sham

sechel

נ = nun ג = gimel ה = hey ש = shin

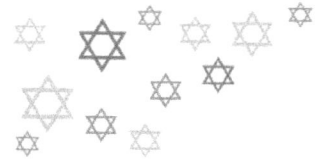
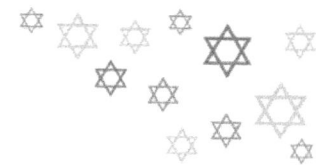

NIGHT 6

EXALTED LIKE SHEPHERDS

On this sixth night of Hanukkah, we once again return to the shamash, the humble servant candle, which sits slightly elevated above the other candles. "You are to be holy to Me, for I, Adonai, am holy, and have set you apart from the peoples, so that you would be Mine" (Leviticus 20:26). This candle, set apart from the rest, should serve as a reminder to strive for holiness, since this is our inheritance as His children. It should also remind us that our humility is not one of position (intentionally lowering or depriving ourselves), but one of submission to Adonai and His Word. He promised us, "when My people, over whom My Name is called, humble themselves and pray and seek My face and turn from their evil ways, then I will hear from heaven and will forgive their sin and will heal their land" (2 Chronicles 7:14). It is in our submission He is best able to display His strength, and it is in meekness we find forgiveness and healing.

In the Hanukkah story, we tell of the Maccabees' self-sacrifice when they risked their lives to rescue and restore the Temple. Even though they defeated a much larger Greek army, their first act was not to celebrate their victory with pride. Rather, they chose submission to Torah and honored their spiritual victory with the rekindling of the Holy Light.

In ancient times, a king of Israel's primary duty was to write for himself a copy of Torah on a scroll so he would remember to keep the law and statutes and not allow his heart to be "exalted above his brothers" (Deuteronomy 17:18-20). Throughout history, we have taught humility to be among our greatest virtues as Adonai's children. We achieve this through submission to His Word, just like the Maccabees.

Looking at the Nativity story, we encounter the lowliest, most humble occupation of the shepherds. Throughout Scripture, Adonai exalts the lowly for His purposes and glory. Jacob was a shepherd who Adonai renamed Israel and gave the legacy of nations. Joseph, a shepherd like his father and brothers, went from the prison to the palace in one day. Moses, while watching his father-in-law's sheep, encountered "I am" in a burning bush on a mountainside, where He called him to deliver Israel from Egyptian captivity (Exodus 3).

Adonai chose Joshua, a man with no authority, to lead Israel into the Promised Land supplied with some of Moses' authority "so that the people of Adonai [would] not be like sheep without a shepherd" (Numbers 27:17-20). Adonai took David from the pasture to the palace (1 Chronicles 17:7). The prophet Jeremiah reiterated he had not "run away from being a shepherd after [Adonai]" (Jeremiah 17:16), and Amos, another prophet, went from following his flocks to prophesying over Israel (Amos 7:14-15).

These shepherds are proof that Adonai "opposes the proud, but gives grace to the humble" (Proverbs 3:34, James 4:6, 1 Peter 5:5). The shepherds in the fields near Bethlehem had nothing to offer the baby Messiah, but after hurrying to see Him for themselves, "they made known the word that had been spoken to them concerning this Child. And all those who heard were amazed at the things the shepherds told them" (Luke 2:17-18).

Like the shepherds, all Adonai asks of us is to come as we are, empty-handed, in humility, and acknowledge Messiah. All we need to offer is a heart of praise and our willingness to share the "Good News...which will be great joy to all the people" (Luke 2:10).

The Word states it best. "Humble yourselves in the sight of Adonai, and He shall lift you up" (James 4:10); "For Adonai takes pleasure in His people. He crowns the humble with salvation" (Psalm 149:4); "The reward of humility and fear of Adonai is riches, honor, and life" (Proverbs 22:4). Humility is the precursor to honor and salvation. Tonight and always, let's humble ourselves before Him, thank Him, and go tell the nations of His precious gift of salvation—*Yeshua.*

Family Discussion Questions

(You may write your answers here or in a journal to compare them year after year. Encourage all family members to take part and reassure them no answer is wrong.)

What does it mean to humble yourself before Adonai?

After winning a competition or prize, what should we do first?

Why was a shepherd's job considered "humble" or lowly?

Do we have to be perfect or righteous to come before Adonai or before accepting Yeshua as our Savior?

Family Prayer Time

(You can use mine or pray in your own words.)

Blessed are you, Adonai our God, King of the Universe and the Lifter of our heads. We thank You for accepting us as we are, with all our flaws, and for loving us without condition or requirement. Help us remember to give You honor and glory in all circumstances, especially when we face success. Teach us to submit to Your Word. Thank you for sending Yeshua as a humble baby to become our salvation. In the name of Yeshua, we pray. Amen.

Unscramble the words below. They all come from tonight's reading if you get stuck.

ANSEVTR _____

RSDEPHEH _____

LHYO _____

UMBLHE _____

OHORN _____

HTROA _____

SEHOPJ _____

CAOBJ _____

MESSO _____

OUJHSA _____

DDVIA _____

IERAJEMH _____

SMOA _____

ASLVANITO _____

Practice copying Torah like the Israelite kings of old. Trace the Hebrew scripture below. Then, memorize it in English and recite it to your family.

"For Adonai takes pleasure in His people. He crowns the humble with salvation."
Psalm 149:4

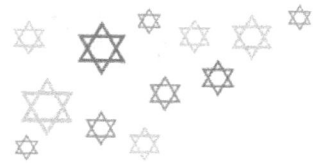
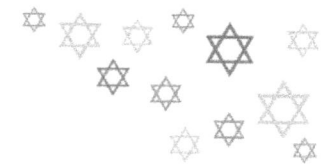

NIGHT 7

BRING OIL LIKE THE LAMB

On this seventh night of Hanukkah, we focus not on the flame but on its source. The oil used to light the menorah has special requirements. In Exodus 27:20, Adonai directed Moses to "command Bnei-Yisrael, that they are to bring to [him] pure olive oil beaten for the light, to cause a lamp to burn continually."

A unique process created this oil. The olives were hand-crushed rather than pressed and then hung in a basket, allowing them to drain naturally. This first bruising and crushing resulted in minimal processing. Filtering removed some of the oil's properties, but allowing it to drain slowly instead, without intervention, made it innately pure. The purest oil produced the best flame and light. This oil only lit the menorah—it had no other purpose. The command states that the people are to bring the oil, implying it is our responsibility to keep our lamps lit as we search scripture and intentionally learn Adonai's truth.

During the Hanukkah story, one flask of this inherently perfect oil refueled the menorah's light. It was only enough for one night, but the miracle story tells of it lasting for eight! This miracle of multiplication took the people through a complete week and into the beginning of the next. When we offer our small portion of faith or obedience, Adonai takes it and multiplies it to last until the next task on the journey He has planned for us. It is our responsibility to replenish our "little" continuously, like the woman with only one jar of oil in 2 Kings 4:1-7, and then offer it up for Him to increase exponentially and perpetually until there is nothing left to contain it.

Last night, we read about the shepherds who left their flocks to seek the One who would bring salvation. But we cannot mention the shepherds without acknowledging the lambs.

These particular animals were important from the beginning for sacrificial purposes. To be acceptable for the *Pesach* (Passover) sacrifice, when the Israelites were preparing for their exodus from Egypt, the lamb had to be without blemish—innately pure, like the first oil from the olives. This lamb provided visible covering for their doorposts from the blood permitted to drain from its sacrificed body. It also offered spiritual protection from death and a way out of the darkness of oppression into the light of Adonai's promise.

Later, in the wilderness, the lamb provided atonement and sanctification (Exodus 29:37-41). Sacrificial lambs redeemed both man and animal (Exodus 34:18-20). In Leviticus, the *kohen* sacrificed spotless lambs for the freewill offerings of atonement, the required guilt offerings to cover intentional sin, and the required sin offerings to cover unintentional misdeeds. The lamb is one of the most important figures from the Nativity story because it represents the Lamb of Adonai, whom He sent to atone for the sin of the world (John 1:29).

"He was pierced because of our transgressions, crushed because of our iniquities. The chastisement for our shalom was upon Him, and by His stripes we are healed. We all like sheep have gone astray. Each of us turned to his own way. So Adonai has laid on Him the iniquity of us all...Like a lamb led to the slaughter, like a sheep before its shearers is silent, so He did not open His mouth" (Isaiah 53:5-7).

Like the olives, our sins crushed Yeshua. Without protest, He poured out His life, His blood, as He hung on the execution stake to cover all Adonai required. "...nearly everything is purified in blood according to the Torah, and apart from the shedding of blood, there is no forgiveness" (Hebrews 9:22). His sacrifice, like the oil carrying fuel through the menorah from its base to its flame, is the tree of Life for us—apart from Him, we die out (John 15:1-5).

Adonai promised, "As a shepherd seeks out his sheep on the day he is among his scattered flock, so I will seek out My sheep. I will rescue them out of all the places where they have been scattered, on a day of cloud and thick darkness" (Ezekiel 34:12).

Tonight, we light the seventh candle in honor of His perfect and complete sacrifice, willingly offered to rescue us from eternal darkness.

Family Discussion Questions

(You may write your answers here or in a journal to compare them year after year. Encourage all family members to take part and reassure them no answer is wrong.)

What are some practical ways we can intentionally learn and grow in truth?

Read & discuss the story in 2 Kings 4:1-7 about the woman and her jar of oil. What is something "small" we can offer to Adonai so He can multiply it?

Why is sacrifice important for us to understand?

Do you believe you need forgiveness? Ask Adonai to rescue you, and then choose to seek and follow His plan for your life.

Family Prayer Time

(You can use mine or pray in your own words.)

Blessed are you, Adonai our God, King of the Universe and the Sacrificial Lamb. Thank You for sending Your Son, Yeshua, to become the pure, final, perfect atonement for our sins. We acknowledge we don't always get it right and often fall short of Your perfect will for our lives. Help us follow Your will over our own. We choose to repent and turn away from wrong so we can walk in Your Truth, Your Light, and Your Way. In the name of Yeshua, we pray. Amen.

Complete and color the dot-to-dot.

He was crushed because of our iniquities.

Isaiah 53:5

Draw a picture of something you can give to Adonai. Write about what you think he might do with your gift. Remember, He takes the little bit we offer and multiplies it into greatness!

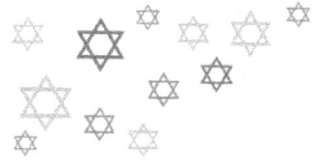
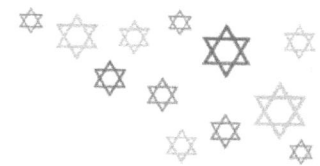

NIGHT 8

OFFER GIFTS LIKE THE MAGI

On the eighth night of Hanukkah, we turn inward and look to the light of life within us. We briefly touched on the eighth letter of the Hebrew alphabet—the letter *chet*—on the first night of Hanukkah.

In Hebraic thought, this letter brings to mind the word *chaim*, which means life. The blood of the lamb on the doorposts on the night of Pesach formed a *chet* and remains a symbol of the sacrificial blood providing life for those set apart because of it. Hebrew is a beautiful language in which each letter holds meaning beyond the sound it makes. *Chet* means "separation" and is a picture of this division of life and death.

In the tabernacle, and later the holy temple, Adonai separated the innermost place, the holy of holies, from everything else. There the *Shekinah*, the glory of Adonai, dwelt. Our innermost being is a holy of holies in the tabernacle of our entire selves. It is here that we invite His Holy Presence to take up residence. "The spirit of man is the lamp of Adonai, searching all his inmost being" (Proverbs 20:27).

In reading the Hanukkah story, we discover the Maccabees separated (*chet*) the spoils of war among the feeble, orphans, widows, and elderly before taking their own shares (2 Maccabees 8:21-29). These gifts of charity show an innermost being, observant of Adonai's commands to care for those who cannot always take care of themselves.

We cannot give from a heart of darkness. Likewise, we cannot worship and shine forth His light from a place of emptiness. There is no irony that the only appointed time in scripture to last for eight days is the Feast of Tabernacles, also known as Sukkot (Numbers 29:35). Sukkot is a time when Adonai fills the Tabernacle with His glory. The Maccabees set a beautiful example of allowing the *Shekinah* to shine from within their bodily temples onto those less fortunate during the eight nights of celebration. We set ourselves apart by gifting His light to others.

When discussing gifts, we cannot forget the riches that traveled from the east to a little boy in Nazareth. Magi came from the east to honor the new king, whose star they had seen. Upon arriving at his home, over which they saw the star once again, "they fell down and worshipped Him. Then, opening their treasures, they presented Him gifts of gold, frankincense, and myrrh" (Matthew 2:11-12).

Some may believe these were simply diplomatic gifts to maintain peace between empires, because they were fine, costly goods from these lands. However, each one holds additional significance when looking at the Word as a whole. The gold, pure and rich, represented the royalty of kings. Frankincense—a pure white oil—took considerable effort and time to harvest, and smelled sweet, but only after applying heat. The Israelites and the *kohanim* added frankincense to the grain offering both when presenting it as a reminder sacrifice, marking it as significant, and when bringing it with their firstfruit offering. Myrrh was also a costly treasure used in the anointing oil created according to Adonai's instructions for setting apart priests and kings. Nicodemus brought myrrh to embalm Yeshua's body before laying Him to rest in a borrowed tomb (John 19:39). These Magi may not have realized the importance or symbolism of these gifts, but we have a bigger picture.

Yeshua is our *Kohen gadol* (our High Priest), the King of Kings and Lord of Lords, who sweetened under pressure like frankincense, "raised from the dead [as] the firstfruits of those who have fallen asleep" (1 Corinthians 15:20), and deserves every offering of remembrance we can give. He said, "As light, I have come into the world, so that everyone who trusts in Me should not remain in darkness" (John 12:46).

As we kindle the final Hanukkah light, take a moment to ensure the gift of Adonai's salvation is lit in your heart, the dwelling place for Him. Yeshua promises, "I am the light of the world. The one who follows Me will no longer walk in darkness, but will have the light of life" (John 8:12).

Family Discussion Questions

(You may write your answers here or in a journal to compare them year after year. Encourage all family members to take part and reassure them no answer is wrong.)

How are our bodies like the tabernacle? Does that affect how we should treat ourselves?

What are some ways we can give to those who are less fortunate?

Why are the gifts from the Magi important?

What is the best gift Adonai gave us? Have you accepted that gift?

Family Prayer Time

(You can use mine or pray in your own words.)

Blessed are you, Adonai our God, King of the Universe and Giver of Salvation. Thank You for the gift of restoration to life you offer us through Yeshua. Your unconditional love and faithfulness in keeping Your promises are worth more than all the praise we can offer in return. Come make Your home in our innermost being, and help us share You with the world. Teach us to be a menorah, shining brightly for all to see. In the name of Yeshua, we pray. Amen.

They presented Him gifts
of gold, frankincense, and
myrrh. Matthew 2:11-12

Color the picture according to the numbers below.

1 = Brown 2 = Pink 3 = Yellow
4 = Orange 5 = Red

# Eight Nights Summary Chart

Night One		
Night Two		
Night Three		
Night Four		
Night Five		
Night Six		
Night Seven		
Night Eight		

Note: See the next page for instructions.

Riding into Jerusalem on the back of a humble donkey, Yeshua started the journey to His end that would give us all a new beginning. Taught to follow Torah in true worship, He honored His earthly father, Joseph, by reigniting the flame of truth. His lineage, through His mother, Mary, carried down Yeshua's authority as High Priest forever, our Redeemer, and our Deliverer-all the way from Adam through servants like Melchizadek, Boaz, and David.

The star announced His birth, but the Light we shine as living menorahs is even brighter. Like the angels, He calls us to share truth boldly, without fear, and to love Him with all our hearts, souls, and strength. Maintaining the meekness of lowly shepherds, we make way for Adonai to set us apart in our words, thoughts, actions, and behaviors. We offer Him the little faith we have like the olive oil for the menorah-pure, sweet, and precious. He takes it and multiplies it through the sacrifice of the Lamb, crushed on our behalf.

The Magi knew of this gift over two thousand years ago. It is the greatest blessing ever presented-the gift of Salvation for all humanity.

Color and cut out each word. Then, glue it on the Eight Nights Summary Chart.

Magi	Salvation for all	gift
multiply	olive oil	lamb
shepherds	set apart	meekness
Shema	share truth	angels
Star	shine Light	menorah
deliverer	high priest	Mary
Joseph	true worship	reignite
humble	new beginning	donkey

Note to parents: You may choose to do this each night to help summarize or at the end of all eight nights for review. The nights are arranged by night from the bottom up for ease in cutting.

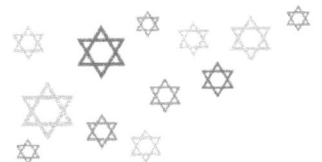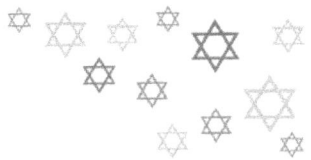

AFTERTHOUGHTS

As you read with your family each night, did you discover anything new? My prayer is for fresh revelation to reach every reader. If that insight led you to discover Yeshua for the first time, let's connect and grow as students of the Word together.

Scripture is clear that belief in Yeshua as Messiah alone is not enough. "The demons also believe—and shudder!" (James 2:19). Yeshua desires a personal relationship with you. If you know Adonai, you will discover you also know Yeshua. You will find Him in the Hebrew letters that craft every word of Torah, hidden in the scriptures written on our hearts, and making up every breath of revelation from the *Ruach HaKodesh* (Holy Spirit).

"You will seek Me and find Me, when you will search for Me with all your heart." (Jeremiah 29:13. See also Matthew 7:7 for reference.)

"Call to Me, and I will answer you—I will tell you great and hidden things, which you do not know." (Jeremiah 33:3. See also 1 Corinthians 2:7-16 for reference.)

If you still seek answers or feel uncertain about the Messianic claims I shared, that's okay. Adonai promises to answer our questions, our seeking, our searching out of His hidden truths—we need only ask. Let's dive deeper into His Word to resolve skepticism and quiet any unrest. My ultimate prayer is for you to draw closer to the heart of the One who created you and loves you infinitely. Everything is meaningless without Him.

If you are convinced Yeshua is the promised Messiah and you desire a relationship with Him, the process is simple. "For if you confess with your mouth that Yeshua is Lord, and believe in your heart that God raised Him from the dead, you will be saved." (Romans 10:9)

That's it. Love Him, walk in His ways, and keep His commandments. Shalom. Shalom.

HEBREW PRONUNCIATION HELPS

Some of the words in this book are transliterated from the Hebrew (such as *shamash*). These are shown in *italics* to set them apart. To help with pronunciation of these words while reading them to your family, please use this chart as a guide.

Hebrew vowels generally have the same sound, unlike their English counterparts.

a—sounds like ah as in water

e—sounds like eh as in elephant

i—sounds like ee as in radio

ei—sounds like ay as in neighbor

ai—sounds like long i as in aisle

u—sounds like oo as in truth

o—sounds like long o as in also

'—sounds like uh, similar to the a in alive

Consonants mostly sound like English with the exception of the following:

tz—sounds like the zz in pizza

ch or kh—sounds like the ch in Bach (P.S. Have fun with the kids by adding a little guttural phlegm sound to this one. They'll sound a bit like cats trying to cough up a hairball, but it makes for excellent fun and endless giggles.)

1. (Melson, 2016)

2. (Shaw, 2015)

3. (Posner, n.d.)

4. (Fruchtenbaum, 2018)

5. (Lanser, 2019)

6. (Sabeny Magazine, 2024)

REFERENCES

Fruchtenbaum, A. (2018, April 20). The Messianic Time Table According to Daniel the Prophet. Retrieved from Jews for Jesus: https://jewsforjesus.org/learn/the-messianic-time-table-according-to-daniel-the-prophet

Lanser, R. (2019, November 16). The Going Forth of Artaxerxes' Decree Part 1. Retrieved from Associates for Biblical Research: https://biblearchaeology.org/abr-projects/the-daniel-9-24-27-project-2/4589-the-going-forth-of-artaxerxes-decree-part1

Melson, R. (2016, April 3). Worship: Our Response to His Greatness. Retrieved from Desiring God: https://www.desiringgod.org/articles/worship-our-response-to-his-greatness

Posner, M. (n.d.). The Story of Melchizedek in the Bible. Retrieved September 24, 2025, from Chabad.org: https://www.chabad.org/library/article_cdo/aid/1326593/jewish/The-Story-of-Melchizedek-in-the-Bible.htm

Sabeny Magazine. (n.d.). Secrets Behind the Dreidel Game. Retrieved December 8, 2024, from Sabeny: https://sabeny.com/sabeny-magazine/secrets-behind-the-dreidel-game-prepare-for-a-game-changer/

Shaw, D. (2015, February 12). Anna of Asher. Retrieved from Theopolis Institute: https://theopolisinstitute.com/anna-of-asher/

ABOUT THE AUTHOR

Amber Whiteaker has a deep passion for highlighting the connections between the old and the new within the Word of Adonai. As an ordained minister, she studies and teaches biblical truths to anyone who desires to learn and grow in their faith. Her heart beats with a special fervor for those who yearn to train up their children in biblical truth. Amber strives to be a true *eshet chayil*, woman of valor, as defined in Proverbs 31. She is an editor, website and graphic designer, and aspiring writer. When she is not freelancing or homeschooling her four precious miracles, you can find Amber digging for diamonds in the Hebraic roots of her faith or snuggling with her sweet husband while watching a rom-com. Be sure to connect with her and watch for new publications at www.amberwhiteaker.com.

www.ingramcontent.com/pod-product-compliance
Lightning Source LLC
Chambersburg PA
CBHW080904120626
46555CB00008B/2952